Good
Character
Traits

Persistence

Ashley Lee

Explore other books at:
WWW.ENGAGEBOOKS.COM

VANCOUVER, B.C.

e WWW.ENGAGEBOOKS.COM

Persistence: Good Character Traits
Lee, Ashley, 1995 –
Text © 2025 Engage Books
Design © 2025 Engage Books

Edited by: A.R. Roumanis
Design by: Mandy Christiansen

Text set in Myriad Pro Regular.
Chapter headings set in Anton.

FIRST EDITION / FIRST PRINTING

LIBRARY AND ARCHIVES CANADA CATALOGUING IN PUBLICATION

Title: Persistence / Ashley Lee.
Names: Lee, Ashley, author.
Description: Series statement: Good Character Traits

ISBN 978-1-77878-739-3 (hardcover)
ISBN 978-1-77878-745-4 (softcover)

This project has been made possible in part by the Government of Canada.

Canadä

Persistence

Contents

What Is Persistence?

Persistence means not giving up when things get hard. It is about trying again and again.

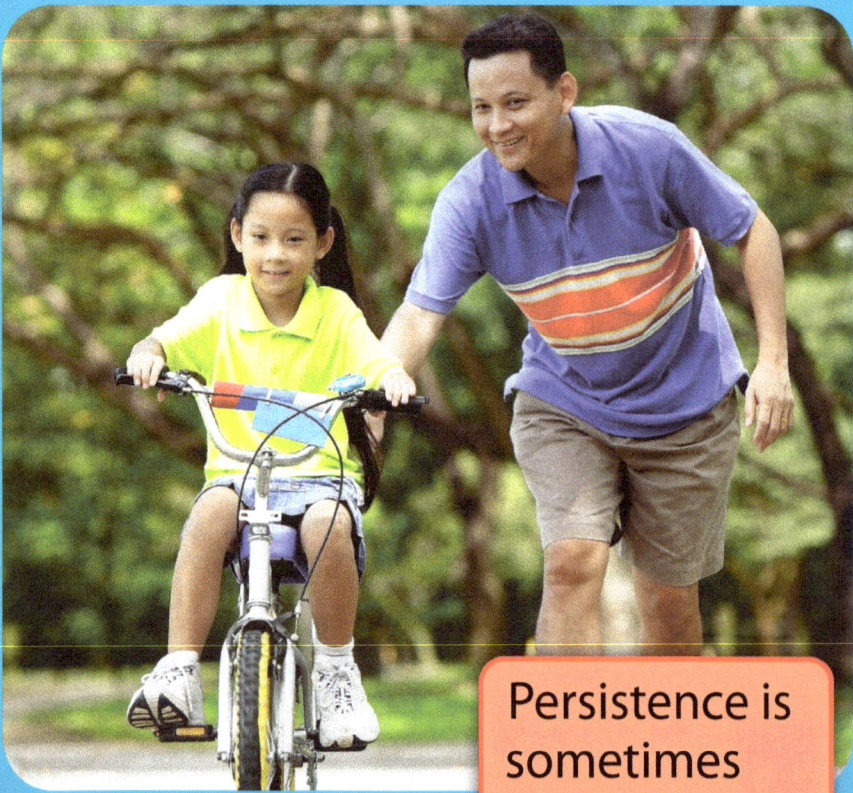

Persistence is sometimes called grit.

Persistence is about believing in yourself. People are more persistent when they really want something.

Why Is Persistence Important?

Persistence helps people work through problems. Working through problems helps them reach their **goals**.

Key Word

Goals: things that people want that they work hard to get.

Persistence helps get things done. There would never be any new **inventions** if people gave up all the time.

Key Word

Inventions: new things that people have made.

What Does Persistence Look Like?

Persistent people do not give up easily. They set goals and keep working towards them.

People who are persistent stay **focused** on what they want. They do not let problems stop them.

Persistent people ask for help when they need it.

Key Word

Focused: pay close attention to something.

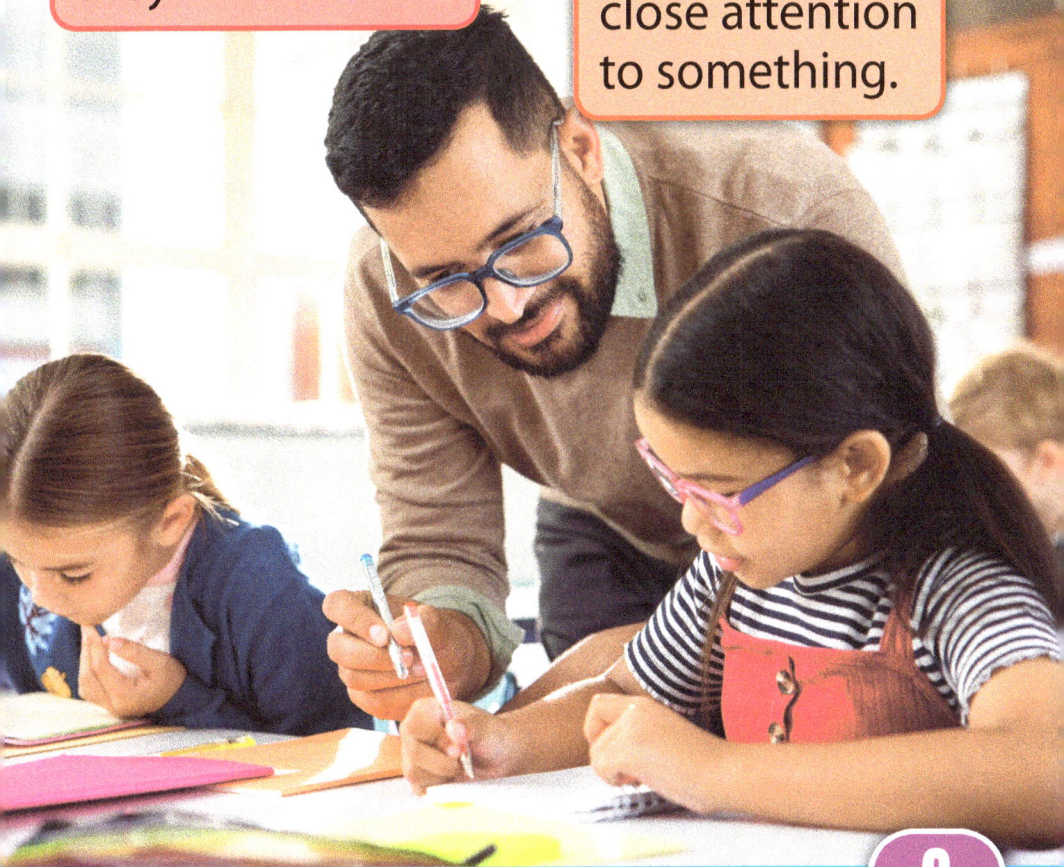

How Does Persistence Affect You?

Persistence helps you learn from your mistakes. It helps you see what went wrong and try something different.

Persistence also helps you to be happier. It feels good to work hard and reach your goals.

How Does Persistence Affect Others?

Persistence can make others want to be persistent too. They want to work hard to reach their goals when they see you reaching yours.

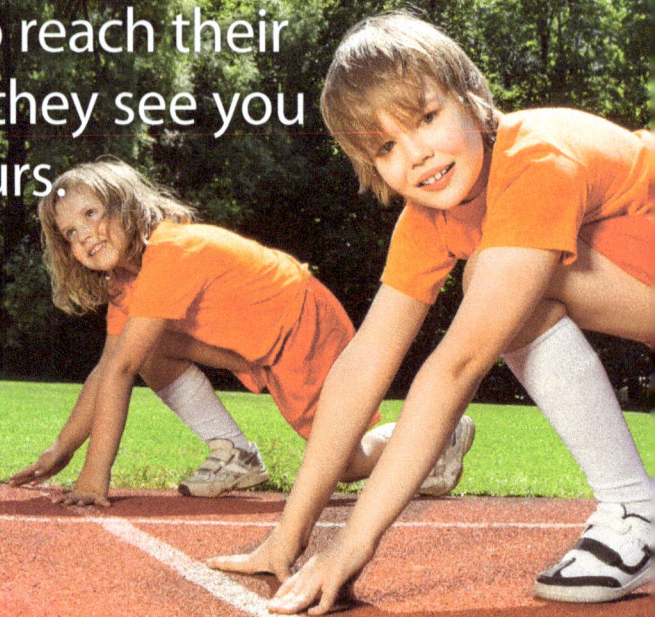

Being persistent can also make others **trust** you more. People are more likely to trust people who try hard.

Key Word

Trust: the feeling that someone is there for you and believes in you.

Is Everyone Persistent?

Not everyone is persistent. Some people are really good at setting a goal and working towards it.

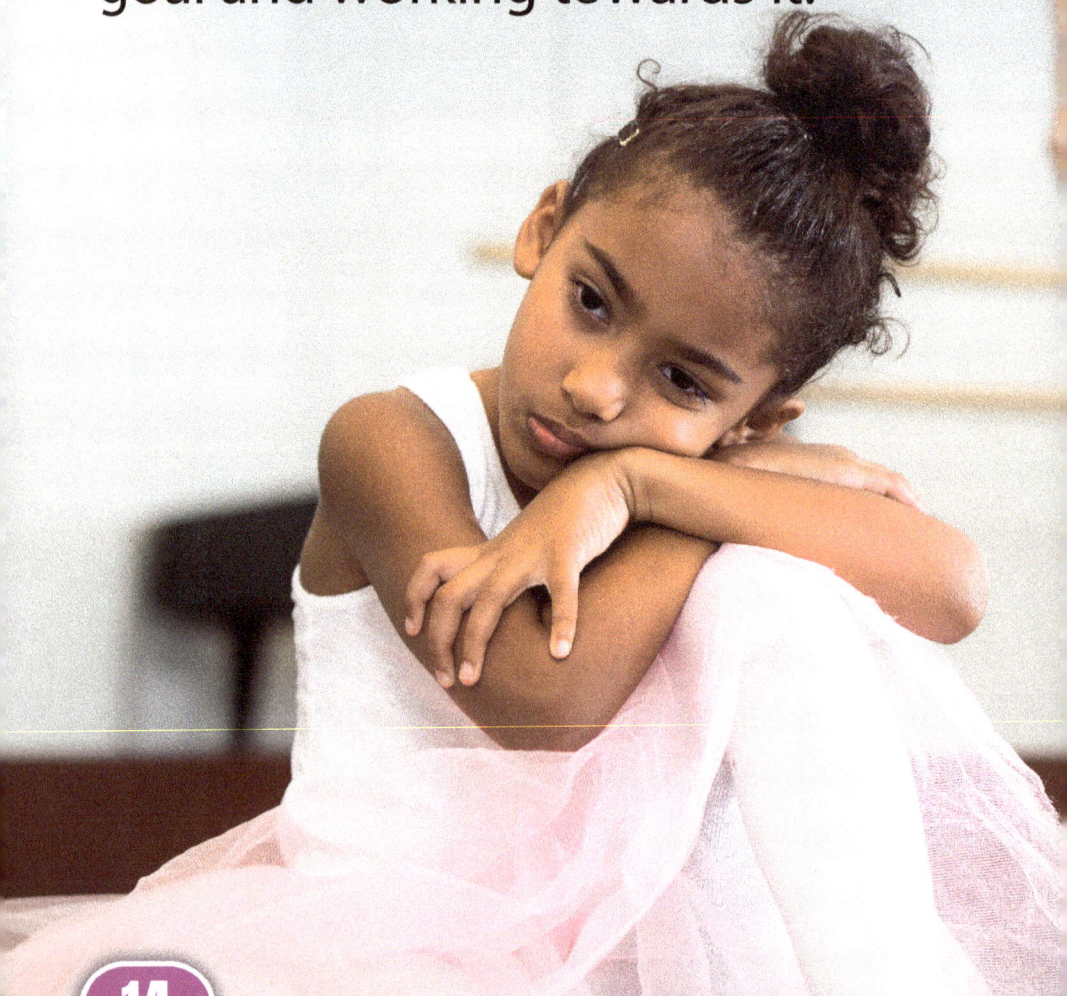

Others might find it easier to give up when they run into problems. But everyone is able to learn persistence.

Is It Bad if You Are Not Persistent?

It is not bad if you are not persistent. But you may have a hard time reaching your goals if you are not persistent.

No one is persistent all the time. Many people are persistent with some things but not others.

It is okay to stop trying if something becomes unsafe.

Does Persistence Change Over Time?

Persistence can get stronger the more you use it. You will work harder to reach your goals when you see that hard work pays off.

People with **mental health** problems may become less persistent over time. They can become more persistent again if they get help.

Key Word

Mental health: the health of your mind.

Is It Hard to Be Persistent?

Being persistent can be hard. It can be even harder when things do not go as planned.

It takes a lot of work to be persistent. But **practicing** persistence will make it easier.

Key Word

Practicing: doing something over and over again to get better at it.

How Can You Learn to Be More Persistent?

Write your goals down and put them where you can see them. This will help you remember what your goals are and why they are important.

Break big tasks into smaller steps. It is easier to work towards finishing small steps instead of one big task.

How Can You Help Others Be More Persistent?

Setbacks can make people forget how far they have come. Remind others of how well they have been doing.

Key Word

Setbacks: things that make it harder for people to reach their goals.

Remind others that setbacks are a part of reaching their goal. Setbacks do not have to be the end of all their hard work.

How to Be Persistent Every Day

1. Start each day with a clear goal in mind.

2. Try to think good thoughts.

3. Remember that even small steps bring you closer to your goal.

4. Take breaks when you need to.

Persistence Around the World

Scientists work hard to make medicines for people. They often have a lot of setbacks.

Not many medicines would
be made without persistence.
Many people would still be sick.

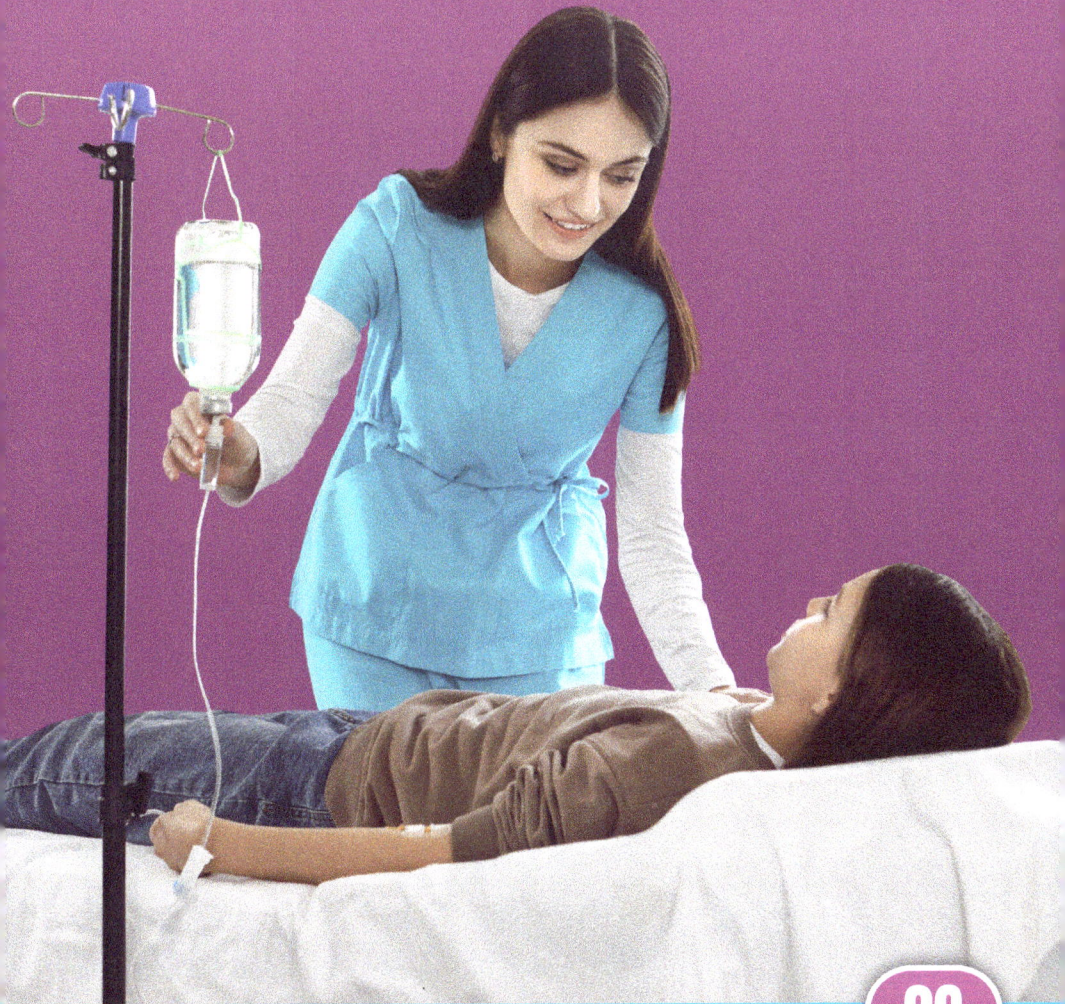

Quiz

Test your knowledge of persistence by answering the following questions. The questions are based on what you have read in this book. The answers are listed on the bottom of the next page.

1 What is persistence sometimes called?

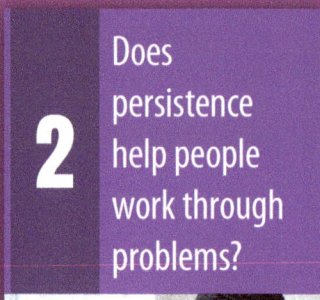

2 Does persistence help people work through problems?

3 Do persistent people give up easily?

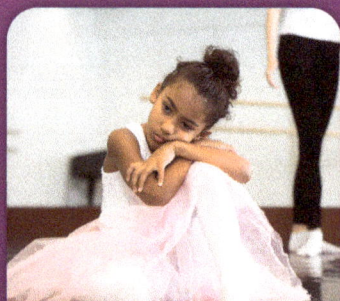

4 Who is able to learn persistence?

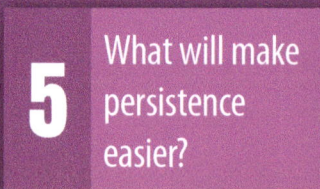

5 What will make persistence easier?

6 What can make people forget how far they have come?

Explore Other Level 2 Readers.

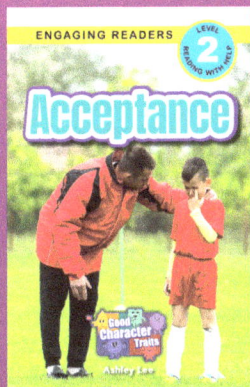

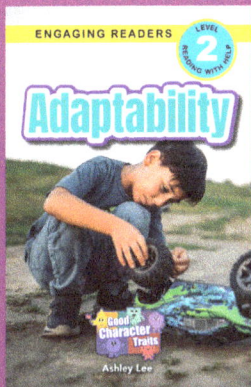

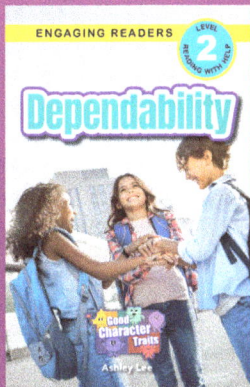

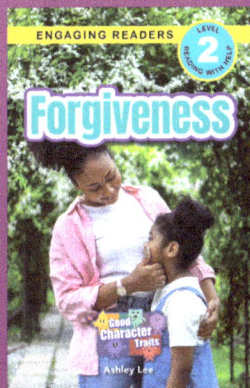

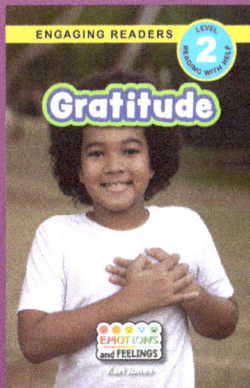

ENGAGING READERS · LEVEL 2 · READING WITH HELP
Acceptance
My Good Character Traits
Ashley Lee

ENGAGING READERS · LEVEL 2 · READING WITH HELP
Adaptability
My Good Character Traits
Ashley Lee

ENGAGING READERS · LEVEL 2 · READING WITH HELP
Dependability
My Good Character Traits
Ashley Lee

ENGAGING READERS · LEVEL 2 · READING WITH HELP
Forgiveness
My Good Character Traits
Ashley Lee

ENGAGING READERS · LEVEL 2 · READING WITH HELP
Humility
My Good Character Traits
Ashley Lee

ENGAGING READERS · LEVEL 2 · READING WITH HELP
Gratitude
EMOTIONS and FEELINGS

ENGAGING READERS · LEVEL 2 · READING WITH HELP
Grief
EMOTIONS and FEELINGS
Sarah Harvey

ENGAGING READERS · LEVEL 2 · READING WITH HELP
Love
EMOTIONS and FEELINGS
Sarah Harvey

ENGAGING READERS · LEVEL 2 · READING WITH HELP
Worry
EMOTIONS and FEELINGS
Sarah Harvey

Visit www.engagebooks.com/readers

Answers: 1. Grit 2. Yes 3. No 4. Everyone 5. Practicing 6. Setbacks